# I'm

# Amazing.

*Rediscovering the joy of being perfectly imperfect*

## Ameila Campbell

ISBN: 978-1-948777-19-3

# DEDICATION

To my dad, the late Charlie Williams: You always loved me for who I was and accepted me for who I was striving to become. Thanks for being my Dad.

To my mom, Mamie A. Williams: Mom you are the most Amazing woman I know; without you, I would not be the Amazing woman that I am.

To my husband, Lorenzo: You brought sunshine into my life; you profess your love for me on a daily basis and provide the sustenance that fuels our relationship. Your protection is that of a king to his queen and I love you for the Amazing man that you are.

To my children, Antwan, Amber, Teryn, Talil, and Treyon: I love each of you for the Amazing individuals that you've become, always remember that you are *enough* and you are *Amazing*.

Thank you for your contribution
to RAIN. We appreciate your
support. You Are Amazing!

I hope you enjoy the Read.

Amy

# Table of Contents

# Introduction

My goal with this book is actually to open up a form of communication and interactive dialogue of communication with other women. There's this tendency to believe that what we've done in our lives is not important or not that great. I desire to help you discover your own joy and look at things differently. I want you to see how things that you thought were meant to destroy you were actually opportunities to grow.

Sometimes moving beyond our negative experiences requires some meditation and candid conversation. This book is not intended to be a quick fix. Instead, it is meant as an interactive medium to help women effectively communicate how we're feeling and what we're going through. As women of power, we are used to commanding stages, winning at the office, and gaining the respect of coworkers while keeping the family together. The tragedy is that we can sometimes look like a public success but feel like a private failure. More often than not, we have few people who can genuinely understand our experiences

We need someone to hear us and validate our stories. Then, we can learn from them and use this knowledge to push us forward into the future. I hope that the transparency and advice found within these pages will help you get there.

Have you ever heard people ask, "What if you passed away? How do you want to be remembered? What do you want people to say about you" If you looked at your life now- at your social media, at things you've done up to this point - would you be satisfied at the story your life is telling?

I have thought about that a lot and decided that if I could sum up my life in one word, it would be "Amazing" and from this well sprung the title of this book, *I'm Amazing*. Of course, things have not been perfect, but that is why this journey has been absolutely Amazing!

My sister, you have an Amazing story. Your life has been paved with pain and promise. Together, let us see the success in our scars - the wonder in our wounds as we emerge victoriously and help other women do the same!

"An olive has to go through three stages, for its oil to run:

It has to go through the shaking, the beating, and the pressing

And just like the olive, some of you may have felt like you go

through the shaking, the beating and the pressing.

You've went through all of that for your oil to flow

Now, your greater is coming...

If it had not been for the shaking,

I never would have been ready for the making, no

If it had not been for the beating,

I would have never knew how anointed I would be.

If it had not been for the pressing,

I wouldn't be able to walk into my destiny."

Excerpt from *"Greater is Coming,"* by Jekalyn Carr

# Chapter 1

# The Fairytale

We have all been through things in our lives that have prepared us for what we were to become. I lay out my story to help you to understand how my upbringing and our society taught me about life:how the fairytales that I saw on television and in books helped me to develop an image of what life and marriage "could" be like.

As a little girl, did you dream about meeting your Prince Charming one day? Did you read those fairytale stories about love and envision the day when your knight in shining armor would whisk you away from your troubles and take you to a land filled with buttercups and roses? For many of us, those fairytales created an image in our minds of what love, relationships, and life should be like.

Through those images, we were taught how to perceive life and our roles within it. Unfortunately, as we grew older, many of us were not shown where the fairytale and reality intersect, causing us to have false expectations and to live a life that is less than what we were meant to have.

As professional women, wives, and mothers, we all have to face challenges and live up to other people's expectations of us. Yet, having never been given the tools and resources to meet those expectations, many of us have failed or stumbled along the way. However, I am here to tell you that you can live the life you have imagined. You can overcome the boundaries and limitations that society has placed on you and on your success and you can achieve all that you desire.

Your life experiences have shaped you into the Amazing woman that you are today. Let's move forward to understand how you can use those experiences to change the lens through which you view life, and use those events as opportunities for growth.

## Marriage

This is where my fairytale begins. Because I had no real examples of what a "good marriage" looked like, I relied on the images that I saw on television to be my guide. I watched as the Huxtable family loved and supported one another. This helped shape my perception of what constituted a good marriage and how I envisioned what marriage would look like for me one day.

I valued the institution and sanctity of marriage. Being raised in the ghetto by a single mother, I could easily have become a statistic: having a child out of wedlock, struggling to raise this baby alone - never happy in a relationship. The odds were all against me, but I still held on to the fairytale. I wanted to be swept off my feet like Sandy in the acclaimed film *Grease*. I longed for my Danny to love me unconditionally, to be dedicated and committed to building a life with me.

Is it so wrong to want a better life and marriage than what you see around you? Although in the community in which I lived (and even in my own home) I did not witness these values or behaviors, I was not satisfied with the status quo. I wanted more. I wanted the fairytale and I was willing to work for it.

In my own home, tragically I witnessed violence, aggression, and rage all too often. When I was very small, my mother threw hot grease at my father, hitting me in the process, leaving not only emotional but physical scars on my body. Certainly, this could not be how two people who love one another behave. I could have easily allowed this type of behavior to taint my views on what love should be. It would have been natural for me to believe that anger and violence were a normal part of marriage because that is what my environment displayed. But I wanted more. I wanted the fairytale.

All too often women repeat this cycle. It is familiar and comfortable to them. Society ingrains this perspective into them, not allowing them to see that there is another way. You may have seen tragedy like this, witnessing abuse, cheating, degradation regularly. Just because you may have seen it does not mean that that will be the life that you lead.

Although I saw this abuse, I was clinging to the idea of romance. I longed for that sense of protection, for a companion who would take care of me and with whom I could spend the rest of my life. I dreamed of being an Amazing mother like Claire Huxtable: a wife, a loving mother, a professional woman. Although this was completely opposite of what I saw around me and what society expected of me, I had a vivid image of what my life, my marriage, and my family would look like.

I was fortunate enough to witness the fairytale in action. It changed my perspective on the real world and gave me hope that I could walk into my fantasy as well. In my teens, I was adopted by an affluent family as part of the Upward Bound program. Although it was not a traditional or legal adoption – more like a mentiorship experience, the opportunity to be paired with a family much different from my own was life-changing. The mom was the epitome of what I envisioned to be a "good wife and mother". She taught me about etiquette and culture, and exposed me to the opportunity to NOT become a product of my environment. She encouraged me that society's perspective on how I should live my life did not have to be reality.

Have you ever had that type of influence in your life? Someone who helped to solidify the image, dreams, and desires in your heart? If you have not yet experienced that, I hope that through my experiences, through my stories, you will be inspired to go after your fairytale as well. Even though you may have seen violence and dysfunction, I can tell you that your fantasy, your vision of what a marriage and unconditional love can be like, is real; it is possible. I walked into my fairytale and you can too!

I was in Germany when I met my first husband. We were both in the military at the time. I was already a single parent and did not want to repeat my mistakes. I had just completed a marriage-counseling program at church where I was asked to write down all the qualities that I thought would embody an ideal husband. When I got to Germany and we met, we connected and it was almost like my dreams had come true. It was love at first sight. He was everything I had envisioned a husband to be. He possessed all of the qualities that I had defined an ideal husband as having.

We were away from family, so there was no pressure, no strings attached. We got to spend a lot of time together, just us. My fairytale did seem possible. When you are starting a new relationship, you know those feelings I am talking about. You are head over heels for the guy, imagining the day that you walk down the aisle together.

Have you ever experienced these feelings? You feel like you are walking on air - like the world is at your fingertips. Everything that you imagined is possible. *Could this be the one who sweeps me off my feet, who will love me unconditionally for the rest of my life?* I wanted the dream and in fact, wanted it to become my reality.

Tory was everything that I had dreamt of and envisioned in my fairytales; he was tall, handsome, well-built, and responsible. Don't forget about a man in uniform!!! He had given up an opportunity to play college football and instead, joined the military to support his two small children back at home. I began helping him financially as I saw how hard he was working to care for his kids.

You may have experienced this in your life. This feeling of total infatuation or lust. You have met this Amazing man. Now what? Is this going to be your dream come true? Maybe this is the beginning of your fairytale? I can tell you that your journey to your dreams may not always be rosy and it will certainly be bumpy. But do not give up hope on your fairytale.

My dream of being a wife was about to come true. We were married in Germany after two and a half years and had built an incredible bond. We had laid an Amazing foundation for the life were returning to. I had a son and he had two children. Sadly, not long after we returned, his daughter's mother passed away. At the age of three, little Amber came to live with us, bringing along with her the baggage that she had already accumulated in her short life.

Do you have baggage? Have you experienced things in your life that you still carry around with you today? Maybe you were the victim of abuse like little Amber. Perhaps you witnessed violence and trauma. Maybe you struggle with self-worth, fitting in, or adhering to culturally defined expectations or rules. Are you allowing your baggage to dictate the direction of your life? Your life is a reflection of your baggage. The decisions you've made up until now indicate if you have been carrying around all that you have gone through and allowing it to predict your future.

I want to tell you that carrying your baggage around with you will serve no purpose other than to weigh you down. Take this opportunity to rid yourself of those things that you experienced that may be preventing you from taking that next step, from achieving all that you were meant to achieve. Through self-reflection, you can identify those things that have been weighing you down and decide if you want to take that baggage with you into your next relationship, your next career move, or even into tomorrow. I had to move past the abuse that I saw as a child so that I could be the best mother possible to my own children.

At any rate, Tory and I had, what I thought, was the perfect nuclear family. It was the family I had envisioned in my fairytale: the loving husband and father leading his family in Bible study. I felt secure in our relationship and I put my faith and trust in him. We had an airtight marriage so I was in disbelief when I finally realized that it wasn't so airtight. My fairytale life was about to be destroyed.

What happens when your dreams fall apart? What do you do when what you think is your fairytale comes crashing down on you? How do you handle what comes next?

You handle it with the same strength and fortitude that you originally pursued your dream with. Do not allow bumps in the road to divert you from your course.

We had been married for six years, moved to Washington State, and had been going to church. Although I had seen signs along the way, I had chosen to ignore them, not wanting to shatter the fairytale life that I was living. My younger sister had come to live with us for a while and she and my husband had had an affair. Not only had my husband cheated but he had crossed the line in having an affair with my sister. My world was starting to crash down around me. I began to question if everything in our "Amazing" marriage and life was a lie.

This part of my story is so therapeutic and healing in a way. I applaud you as the reader for your vulnerability if you are reading this thinking, "Yes, that is me. That happened to me too." It is so important that we realize as women that we're not alone. So that's why this part of my story is for you as much as for me.

You need to stand *on* your story, not *in* your story. Do not allow what has happened to you to define you going forward. You have to shake off the dirt of those things that were meant to kill you and use them to propel your life to the next level. I hope that my courage in sharing my experiences is going to allow a woman who is going through something right now to feel like she has a sister and that she doesn't have to hide from it or be ashamed because of it. It is my sincere desire that my testimony gives hope to someone who feels like they are in a pool of darkness and just treading water, getting nowhere.

In the next pages, I will talk specifically to you if you find yourself in this position or in any circumstance that goes against what you envisioned your life to be. If you are experiencing this breakdown in your fairytale, I will share what things worked for me.

I had to accept that my husband's affair was a bump in our marriage, in my fairytale. A speedbump that I had not seen coming but was prepared to handle because I had been growing spiritually. We were growing spiritually as a family so I did what I knew to do – I went to God.

I learned the importance of the power of faith and forgiveness. Before this critical time in my life, forgiveness was just an act. I had to deal with betrayal and pain on an indescribable level. Although the pain of his indiscretions was like a punch in the gut, I forgave him right away; the only comfort that I knew I could find was in God. At that moment, I had to spiritually connect with God to get me through. On my knees, I felt the love and the embrace of the Holy Spirit helping me keep it together. I believe the act of forgiveness opened the door for my healing to begin immediately.

Spiritual growth came to me once I was able to see how to take responsibility for my actions and the error of my ways through scripture. We've all heard it before. Women who go through or survive cheating affairs should not blame themselves. However, I realized that

I was to blame for his affair. I had put my husband before God. In my desire to live my fairytale life, I had set expectations for how I wanted him to behave and live; however, he couldn't meet them. Everything that I thought I wanted and needed from him I should have been seeking from God.

It takes a lot of spiritual maturity to recognize and admit all that happened to me. As many of you out there, I witnessed both physical and verbal abuse yet I held on to my dream of having a fairytale marriage. I met my Prince Charming, my Cliff Huxtable. I was happy until my world came crashing down with betrayal and I realized that I had based my marriage on fantasy alone. To any of you who may have experienced this as well, the shattering of your fairytale dream, I am here to tell you that you must and will get to the point where you can look in the mirror and say, "I Am Enough!"

I realized that I was not alone in my struggle. For so many years, I had supported my husband while putting my own needs aside and suffering in silence. If you have ever watched *T.I. & Tiny: Friends & Family Hustle*, you will see that women from all walks of life are faced with this same struggle. In the very first episode of the season, Tiny confronts T.I. about his cheating ways even though they are supposedly working on their marriage. He refuses to change although he professes his love for her. Sound familiar? Anyone out there experience this same situation? Your man expects you to stand by and stand with him despite his faults.

While many label the ability to swallow their own emotional needs as resilience (and take pride in it) whom is it helping in the end? Unfortunately, society has perpetuated the fairytale for women of color for so long that we have to deal with it for the sake of our marriage; many of us stay "stuck" in it for far too long.

Even though I was growing stronger spiritually, my confidence had been shaken to the core and my self-worth and self-esteem were the first to be trampled underfoot. I was full of regret and remorse. I should have been able to let go of the vision that I had for my life and understand that "I Am Enough", but this was proving easier said than done.

I began rediscovering things about myself that I had lost along the way. I had given up working to become a full-time mom; so, I began refocusing on my career. I had stopped taking care of myself; so, I started working out. I began working on the outside and the inside, looking for opportunities to be better.

If you have been struggling, get back to knowing God and yourself again. Remind yourself of who He says you are. One of the scriptures that reassures me is Romans 8:28, "And we know that all things work together for good to those who love God, to those who are called according to *His* purpose."

You are enough and have to fall in love with YOU again.

Many of us have created this image in our minds about what marriage should be like and society has helped us to develop the fairytale perspective. I am here to tell you that you will get through and you can live the fairytale life that you have dreamt of. It may be difficult and you will go through ups and downs, but you will prevail. The true test will be in how you bounce back from the trials and tribulations that life brings you, putting your faith in God and trust in yourself.

Brenda Braxton, the owner of BBraxton, Exceptional Grooming for Exceptional Men, knows a little something about trials and tribulations. After being forced to dissolve her business due to mismanagement by her business partners, she learned several valuable lessons about business and bouncing back, including resilience, believing in yourself, learning from your mistakes, working hard, and most importantly, putting your faith in God. To carry her through the difficult times and to give her strength to put one foot in front of the other, she refers to Psalm 46:10 which states, "Be Still and Know That

I am God".

In the next chapters, I will break down the process of rediscovering your joy and living out your dreams!

# Chapter 2

# Imposter Syndrome

Although it may be difficult and uncomfortable to talk about emotions and memories, it is the best way to remind ourselves of the strength, courage, and wisdom that we have gained along the way. Evaluating where you have been inspires you to keep moving forward.

You may have heard about the mask that many of us carry around with us. The mask that is placed or rather forced on us in different stages of relationships and at different times in our lives. This mask turns us into an imposter in our own lives. According to Gill Corkindale's article, "Overcoming Imposter Syndrome" published in the Harvard Business Review, impostor syndrome is defined as a collection of feelings of inadequacy that persist despite evidence of success. It includes feelings of self-doubt and a sense of being a fraud all while experiencing exceptional public success.

Unfortunately, imposter syndrome is not unique to one particular gender, group, industry, education level, or socioeconomic status. It can affect everyone at some point in their lives. There is research, however, to support the idea that it tends to hit minority women harder than others. According to Kevin Cokley, a professor of educational psychology and African diaspora studies at the University of Texas at Austin, "a lack of representation can make minorities feel like outsiders, and discrimination creates even more stress and anxiety when coupled with impostorism."

For example, Issa Rae, the star and co-creator of the HBO Series "Insecure", shares how Hollywood disproportionately represents women and minorities, causing her to battle with imposter syndrome herself. In her book, *The Misadventures of Awkward Black Girl,* Ms. Rae tells the audience that the "universal gender classification for *girl* is white" and therefore, acceptable to the world. Are we, as beautiful black women, supposed to live up to this representation of what a girl or woman is supposed to be? Absolutely not! The views of society have tried to pigeonhole us into who we are supposed to be rather than who we are.

Author and inspirational journalist Jolie A. Doggett tells of her struggle with imposter syndrome. Although many people say that she inspires them with stories that matter to her, as a Black woman, she struggles with the feeling that someday someone will pull back the curtain on her to reveal her as an "untalented hack". She feels like a fraud and in her own head, tells herself that she is not good enough to be complimented for her work or that she is, at every moment, on the verge of plummeting off the cliff into failure. "For people of color, imposter syndrome isn't just an imaginary voice in our heads. We receive almost daily messages from society that we don't truly belong."

My goal in this chapter is to help you to understand how to identify when you are being an imposter. We tend not to realize it until it's too late, which is a true tragedy. You may become who you knew you were supposed to be, but sometimes it's at the peril of a relationship role, such as a spouse or even a parent.[i]

## An imposter wife

The mask I was wearing in my first marriage to Tory was that of the ideal wife based on the fairytale I had envisioned. While I appeared to be the perfect wife in public, I felt inadequate deep down in my heart. Looking back after all that has happened, I realize that I was, in fact, the victim of the imposter syndrome. In other words, I felt inadequate although, by all accounts, my marriage appeared to be happy and healthy from the outside.

Sometimes we wear the mask, putting our own needs and wants to the side because we believe it will please others. I played the imposter role as I played the perfect" wife, having the perfect marriage, suppressing my feelings, my desires, and neglecting my relationship with God. I felt as though I had to live up to my own self-imposed expectations for how a relationship and marriage should be and to achieve it, I had to be someone that I wasn't.

We all have certainly felt like a fraud in our relationships and even in our own homes at some point in our lives. Think about a time when you were not being true to yourself and instead, catered to how you thought the other person expected you to act or think. You are not alone. Although the point of my stories is to tell you how and when I was an imposter, it is also to demonstrate how I was able to take off the mask and find myself once again. As I mentioned previously, I had to go back to God as my source of strength and to learn to forgive both my husband and myself.

From the beginning, I pampered him. I paid his child support for him; I took him out to eat; I gave him money when he needed it. I helped him live comfortably, all in the attempt to make him see that I was a good wife. Although I had been the power broker in the situation before we were married, I gave up my power once we signed the papers. I had now put on the mask, posing as a doting, overly indulgent, caring wife. In fact, the perfect wife, by my own definition.

Ultimately, by being an imposter, I had only hurt myself. My husband did not recognize that I was being anything other than my natural self because he married the same person I had always been WITH him. He married the woman who wanted the perfect marriage, the fairytale image of the perfect wife. So, for him, his treatment of me over the years was justifiable since I had been so accommodating.

It should have been no surprise that when he announced that he was going into the ministry and preaching his first sermon, he did not invite me to the service. I should not have been amazed when he called his mother to invite her and praised her for her continuous support over the years. I should not have been shocked when he neglected to thank me for being instrumental in his life. What was shocking to me was that I had allowed myself to be used as a doormat for so many years.

Who was this woman who neglected her time with God, who stopped caring about her appearance, who had stopped loving herself, yet expected her husband to love her? I had stopped looking in the mirror and saying "I AM Enough!" I certainly did not recognize this imposter who was staring back at me.

Have you ever felt that you were pretending to be someone that you are not? If you know who God has intended you to be and yet you are not walking in that vision, you need to get back to His desire for your life. Although my journey in my first marriage was what I thought was my fairytale, in fact, I was simply posing as someone other than who God intended for me to be. At this point in my life, I still had not realized it yet. I want to pause here to tell you not to beat yourself up or feel ashamed if you have gone through something similar. It is time to forgive yourself and step out into all that God has intended for you to be.

Time and time again I saw signs of how my husband took me for granted. On the other hand, I did not see at the time how my desire to be the perfect wife had put my own sanity and happiness in jeopardy. I had fallen victim to male privilege and more specifically, black male privilege, but did not even realize it. This double standard in which men believe to have superiority over black women trapped me in my own thoughts, beliefs, and even my time with God. I hope that by sharing my stories you will see the error in your ways and make the change before you have to experience the trials and challenges that I did.

Moving forward, not long after he was called into ministry, Tory was offered a highly esteemed opportunity to join the Reserve Officer Training Course (ROTC). Being the supportive, perfect wife that I was, I encouraged him to interview and, in fact, accept the position, once again putting my own needs aside again. While he spent two and a half years training for the program, I worked multiple jobs, took care of the family, and cared for our disabled son. He was my husband and, in my mind, I was only doing what was necessary to keep our family together and to be a good wife.

When he got commissioned as an officer, there was a big ceremony to celebrate his accomplishments. Once again, he called his mother, acknowledged her unending encouragement, and even thanked our children for their support during the journey. Again, I was disappointed in his lack of consideration or acknowledgment of me. Should I have been surprised? Didn't I learn previously who he was and what disillusion I had been living under? I accept the fact that I created this situation by placing his needs always above my own and certainly in front of God. But, at this point in my life, I believed we had a good marriage.

My sister, do you see how my dreams of living the fairytale life had prevented me from truly living the life I desired? All was not lost though, and, in the end, you will see how everything came full-circle for me and it will for you as well.

Aside from his affair, my husband had already demonstrated to me over and over again how my fairytale was purely in my own imagination. From the ministry to the ROTC, he had proven time and time again who he was. Yet I still kept expecting him to change when in fact, I should have been the one to change, to remove my mask, to live the life of my dreams.

Again I was surprised at his behavior when suddenly I was the one who needed something. After going to the hospital several times, I was finally admitted for an emergency appendectomy. Yes, my sweet ladies, my appendix had erupted. I was gravely ill and was getting sicker. After three days, I was supposed to be going home, however the doctor admitted to my husband that something was wrong.

Although Tory was supposed to be going to Iraq, his commanding officer ordered him to stay with me as his place of duty. Several months and many surgeries later, I learned that the surgeon had nicked a blood vessel in my abdomen during the surgery, causing massive internal bleeding. It wasn't the trauma of surgeries or loss of blood that was causing me pain. Unfortunately, it was my husband's lack of concern and downright neglect that hurt me to the core. Each time I asked him to visit me or bring the children to the hospital, he had an attitude as if I was an inconvenience to him, an interruption in his life.

I was nowhere near out of the woods and doctors had told him that I had a long road ahead of me. It was during this time when I was in the hospital that it hit me. He didn't care! Even when he did come, he would flirt with all of the nurses. Of course, I knew the signs. Remember I had fallen for those same tricks many years before. This was the final straw. Lying there in my hospital bed, not certain of my fate, it all was very clear to me.

We have all been there. I am sure you have experienced a time when you finally have had enough and are ready to move on. You finally realize that you have been lying to yourself, possibly for years, doing your best to keep up the image, all the while telling yourself stories that you actually came to believe. What do you do when you ultimately recognize those lies that you have been telling yourself for what they truly are?

As women, we are all faced with many mental battles. The battle lies between who people, like our husbands and children, expect us to be, and the reality of who we know God created us to be as our authentic selves. This may be difficult to wrap your mind around. However, I am here to tell you that you can overcome imposter syndrome. You can live your best life and be who God intended for you to be.

Mentally you suffer in different ways. Even though I thought I was forgiving, it was in fact just self-sabotaging. My body was badly scarred but I knew what I had to do once I was healthy again. While I was in for one of my many bandage changes, I joked with the surgeon about his friend, the plastic surgeon. "Can he give me some implants because I'm going to need something to help me get a new husband?"

Although I was joking about the implants, I was very serious about the husband. Again, thoughts of my inadequacies sneaked in. I began thinking about what people would say about a single woman with all these kids; what will I do? Who will want me with all of these scars? The mental anguish of still trying to wear my mask had enslaved me within my own mind.

I prayed to God. I asked him to please give me strength. What was I praying for? What strength was I looking for? Was I asking for him to help me continue with the charade that I had been living or to help me to move on, to divorce my husband, and start fresh? To be able to hear the answer, I had to first get to know and love myself.

I had a new determination about me. Nothing was going to stop me now. I knew what I had to do and in fact, I scheduled an interview while I was still in the hospital. Because of my credentials, they held the job for me. Leaving the hospital, I headed straight to the interview.

They had no idea what to expect and frankly, neither did I. I think they were more impressed with the fact that I came straight from the hospital and was still able to laugh at myself. I got the job, which was the beginning of an entirely new journey in my life.

It was during this very difficult time in my life that I learned a very important lesson that I must pass on to you. In this tug of war that we all experience between our reality and our expectations, it is critical to laugh more than you cry, to make up your mind when you see the signs, and make that next move your best move. Of course, that is all much easier said than done. The battle going on in your mind is going to be harder than the physical battle of life that you are facing.

I stopped focusing on the pain and the scars and instead focused on the healing and being whole. I looked at life through an entirely new lens. I had to ask myself, as important as marriage is to me, do I want to be married to *this* person?

This was the first of many sobering questions I had to ask myself, which led me to do a reality check. I began focusing on my career, putting my children first, and I stopped trying to please others. I began to love myself again.

For many of us, we hesitate to ask ourselves those tough questions. In the next chapter, we will look at how to do a full inventory of your gifts and talents and make sure you do a complete check on reality so that you fall in love with yourself again.

## An imposter parent

My son, Talil, was born as an identical twin with myelomeningocele, more commonly known as spina bifida. What that means is that his spine did not completely form (or close) at birth, the way it should have. The doctors could not tell us the extent of his issues or what to expect, other than he would be paralyzed from the waist down. This is when my spiritual journey began.

During a heart to heart meeting with God, He showed me what Talil's future would be. I saw him walking despite what the doctors had told me. It was when I first tried to breastfeed him that I realized how strong I had to be for him. He was so fragile and his feet were severely deformed, yet I knew that God had selected me to be his mother for a reason.

I got out of the military and focused all of my attention on helping Talil to have all of the opportunities in life just like the other kids. I helped him do all the things that the doctors told me he would never do: walk, ride a bicycle, ice skate. He even played the Bass Drum in his high school marching band!

Being a twin, I knew each of the milestones that he should have reached. His brother was crawling, walking, and talking while Talil was not even attempting any of these things. The harder that I tried to make him stand, the more determined he was to NOT stand up. That is when I decided that Talil would no longer get any special treatment. A disability to me means that there are limitations and I had accepted that he was disabled. Until I decided to change my mind. Talil just needed to believe that he could do it. I think maybe we all had been listening to the lies that we had been telling ourselves.

Once I began to treat Talil like the other kids, using the same punishment and motivations, he began to walk. I began to tell him to develop a new set of expectations. You are not disabled; you are not handicapped, I would tell him. Sure, you may not look the same, but you can still do anything you set your mind to.

Talil taught me so much about determination and having a strong, positive mindset. I was tough on him and it paid off. Each time that we went back to the doctors, they were amazed at his progress. They could not believe he was standing let alone walking. They started looking at me as if I was the typical crazy nutcase mom. They thought I was in denial of my son's situation when in fact I saw what they saw, but I also knew what I saw beyond what they were looking at.

It was difficult. Like many of you who are faced with challenges, I was often at my breaking point. But my faith carried me through. I was believing in God- that He would give me what I needed to be strong. I just knew that anything was possible for Talil. When I think about those dark days, I recall saying to myself, "With man this is impossible, but with God all things are possible" (Matt. 19:26).

I always tried to live up to being the perfect parent. Doing everything for my kids, sacrificing everything if need be. But was I an imposter parent? Was the concern with how doctors and passersby would view my family greater than my actual concern for my children?

If you are a parent then you know what I am talking about when I say imposter parent. Parenting is difficult and no, we do not always make the best or right decisions for our children. But this is where doubt creeps in and tells you that you are an imposter, that you are failing your children, or that you setting them up to fail. I want to reassure you that no parent will ever make EVERY right decision; no parent will leave this earth thinking that they did an absolutely Amazing job in raising their children because no one is perfect.

Yes, you will do your best to instill values, morals, and ethics. You will teach them to be kind, gracious, generous, and to love God. But, will you be the perfect parent? No. No one is, Do not let anyone or any situation make you feel less than, that you are not doing a good job raising your children. Do not let anyone place doubt in your mind. You will not be the first person to let your baby sit in a dirty diaper too long or allow your teen driver to be out past curfew. You certainly will not be the only person in the world to use corporal punishment and in fact, you may even get a few shouts of "Amen Sister" for it!

Do your best for your children, but do not expect to be the perfect parent. You will only be setting yourself for the trap of the imposter parent syndrome. Remember that the only perfect parent is our one and only loving Father: God Himself.

When we first came to Washington State, Talil needed to have surgery to reposition a shunt in his brain.. Although a standard procedure for children with his condition, it was still brain surgery and I was nervous. He came out of the surgery completely fine, but he had this big bandage wrapped around his tiny head and casts on his feet. I remember pushing him around in the stroller next to his twin, wondering what the people who passed were thinking, imagining that their looks were shaming me. Were they really or was this just another lie that I was telling myself?

When we show up to be the superheroes of our families- the mothers, the wives, the sisters, the aunties that our family need us to be - sometimes we are not mentally prepared for how exhausting that experience can be. It requires mental tenacity, a mindset of strength. You have to get through the weak moments to get the strength to perform with excellence.

I learned to not look at everything with my physical eyes. I had to see beyond where we were. Looking beyond the condition that he was born with was difficult for everyone but I learned to look at where he was going. He was purposeful. I knew that in my own strength I couldn't do it. I had to rely on God's supreme wisdom and the knowledge that there is a bigger purpose beyond my current situation. When I prayed about the situation, God showed me that ultimately we're all God's children and God entrusted Talil in my care and I took that very seriously. He had entrusted this precious child in my care. The disability was a blessing; God believed in me more than I believed in myself. He knew that I would be the person who could get out of myself for a moment to invest in someone else at a critical point in their life.

God showed me that there was more to life than what I had been searching after. I was really ambitious and driven. I was into this marriage and everything that came with it. When Talil was born, I had to ask myself what is important. I could have asked why this was happening to me, but who else was going to do it? If not me, then who?

God wants you to see your burden as a blessing. It is all about the perspective that you have on it. If you are currently experiencing difficulty, remember that He will never give you more than you can bear. God thinks a lot of you to entrust you in your particular circumstance. It is a privilege and takes spiritual maturity to recognize this.

# Chapter 3

# Reality Check: Seasons of Womanhood

## Reality Check

Coming to grips with who you are and your imperfections is an important part of the process which I will call the "reality check". There are going to be days when although you try to be the superhero of the moment, when you want to be the person who can handle it all, you crumble.

When my first husband and I got married, he already had two kids and I had one. We came back after our tour in Germany to my first reality check. One of the first calls that we received was from his daughter's mom. She was in the hospital and was, in fact, very ill. I met her over the phone and had a lot of respect for her.

When she saw me, we hugged like sisters. Knowing how sick she was and thinking ahead for her daughter's well-being, she asked me if we would take her daughter, Amber, home with us. At almost three, Amber had already been with many different people in the family. All Amber's mother wanted was to know that Amber would be safe.

Unfortunately, when I finally got to meet Amber, she looked as if she had been thrown away; her hair was a tangled mess, she was in desperate need of a bath, and her clothes were old and dirty. The reality and gravity of this little girl's situation struck me like a slap to the face. Someone had done something horrible to this baby even at her young age. Whether it had been sexual or not was hard to tell and she was too young to tell me. My heart broke as I washed the dirt from her body and watched as she froze every time my husband - her father - walked into the room. Just as she began to trust me, her mom, unfortunately, passed away. My world had just grown by one.

Although I tried to convince my husband that we had to take this precious little one to the hospital for an evaluation, he was concerned about what people would think. He did not want anyone to think that we had done something to her. So, despite my best efforts to comfort her and relieve any guilt on her part, little Amber struggled with what she had already experienced in her short life. She and I bonded over the next few years, but at that time, still having a distrust of men, her relationship with her father a was strained one.

Unfortunately, this created a divide between my husband and me that eventually placed an irreparable wedge between Amber and me later on. His jealousy over our relationship led him to take her away from me as we were going through the divorce. I never thought of her as anything other than MY daughter, so when this happened, it sucked the life out of me.

All of those years when I was caring for Amber and we were growing closer, he let me believe that she was my daughter because it was benefiting him. The reality of it was that she was a part of my fairytale. It was convenient for him. He was used to me taking care of him and it was only natural that I would take care of his children too. For me, she was a little girl who I fell in love with.

While my husband was deciding that he wanted to be a geographical bachelor and we began the separation process, I was called to Iraq. All of the children moved to Oregon to live with him during the two years that I was expected to be gone. This was going to be a huge sacrifice for me. I was going to be putting my life on the line every single day while I had to trust that he would care for our children.

Before the days of cell phones, I received regular letters from him about mundane, trivial child-rearing things. Here I was in the most dangerous place in the world at the time, putting myself in harm's way, and he couldn't handle being a dad. But that tells you how absent he had been from the relationship for so long; he couldn't handle basic things. Unfortunately, while I was gone, although I had been writing them letters, he was sowing seeds amongst my children against me.

When I returned, everything was different. The moment I landed back on U.S. soil, the first thing I did was borrow a stranger's phone to call my husband to tell him that I was back and coming to get my kids. I was immediately smacked with a dose of reality when he told me that Treyon was missing. He had either run away or was taken by social services. What!?! When I got home, I realized that the situation was even worse. Talil was in a wheelchair and Amber was now referring to me as "that woman". What had he been doing and telling my children all of this time? Had they received any of my letters? While I was deployed, the children also learned that they had another brother. What a way to find out - from the taunting of kids at school. "Hey, your dad is my brother's dad!" Was this any way to raise children?

I should have been coming home celebrated as a hero like the other veterans. Instead, my world was crumbling. I had to take off the mask and see life for what it was.

While we want to experience the fairytale life, we also have to understand the reality of it. Sometimes we have to be a superhero at the most inconvenient times. I had to step out of one life-threatening situation and walk directly into another. Although my life was not in danger back home, my confidence, my emotions, and my fairytale were now in harm's way. Abandonment, betrayal, and fear all crept back in.

Have you ever realized that when you took off the mask, life was not what you expected? You may wonder how you got to this place, this reality. As women, we go through different stages in our lives, different seasons and many people transition in and out of these seasons with us.

You may be questioning how to manage keeping in tune with yourself and with who God intended for you to be during these different ebbs and flows of life? How are you able to place faith above fear in these seasons of transition? Your faith will be tested and you will be fearful as you experience both the fairytale and the reality. But hang tight because you will get through. You will prevail and you will experience joy in your life.

## Seasons of Womanhood

We all experience various seasons of becoming a woman and seasons of life. Each season brings with it its own challenges and advantages.

Yet God has already laid out the plan for your life in anticipation of its bumps and bruises because He knows that you are a woman of noble character, deserving of all of His blessings.

## Winter season

The winter season for me is the time of storing up and building. While everything is slower during this season, this is the time to take advantage of and celebrate the small things in life. It may seem harder to see the blessings in the wintertime but remember that they are there and you need to show gratitude for all of them, as challenging as this may be.

Winter can be cold and lonely. For many women, depression can be born out of this sad place and time in our lives. There is a reality to this season that can be difficult to accept, yet everyone experiences a winter season at some point in their life. Remember that after the winter always comes the spring!

I consider my deployment to Iraq to be a winter season in my life. I had already experienced a rebuilding after the emergency appendectomy. I was stronger, more self-aware, and certainly smarter. I had built myself up and removed the mask that I had been wearing for so many years.

Now it was time for me to go and be strong. I had spent a lot of time in the military preparing soldiers to go to war. It was my turn to implement all that I knew to stay alive.

Although it had been six years since my many surgeries and bouts with anemia, my body was vulnerable. My doctors were hesitant to clear me for deployment, but as a black woman in an officer's position in the military, I knew that I could not give them any reason to think that I was backing down.

It took a lot of faith to really trust God. The truth of the matter is, I knew there was a possibility I wouldn't come back home. My new reality was going to be one of extremely harsh conditions in the worst, most violent place to be. I was the highest-ranking female officer deployed in this unit.and I am black. They didn't even know what to do with me.

At first, I was looked at as a joke. I had to really struggle to maintain my professionalism. No one within my command took me seriously, even so far as cursing and disrespecting me. For example, I received a gift on my birthday. Someone sent me balloons and after picking them up, my second in command, a seasoned military man, yelled and screamed about how distracting the balloons were, and that I should get out of the vehicle and walk. Through his actions and words, he had made it very clear that he did not want to work with me. To make matters worse, I outranked him. No matter what, I had to maintain my professionalism.

When we returned to the base, I spoke with my superior and asked to bring him up on disciplinary action for disrespecting an officer. This was certainly not how I wanted to start off working with my team. The senior officer tried to defend him, telling me that he had been around for a long time. As a woman, I had to lay the foundation to be respected in my role.

Especially, as a black woman; we always seem to have to defend our right to be respected. Do you sometimes feel that you are given much less respect and recognition than you deserve?

I had worked so hard to earn my rank as an officer and I was not going to allow this guy to disrespect another officer in uniform, no matter what his personal feelings were about me. Disrespect was simply not going to be tolerated. We agreed to settle it but of course, he did not apologize.

Because of my background, I've always maintained confidence in my competency. When I arrived in Iraq, I was the only trained logistical officer that they had. They were a fighting artillery unit. This was an all-male unit used to fighting with big guns. Yet, I was the most experienced officer in my career field and it showed. In addition to serving as the primary Logistics Officer, I was the only certified military test control officer in Iraq at the time. In other words, I was qualified to administer and evaluate a multi-part assessment used by the military to identify individual aptitudes and areas of greatest career potential. By the time I arrived, they had sought me out.

Although the base is very secure (like a fortress), as a test officer, I had to travel around the entire battlefield administering various exams. For example, if someone wanted to take on a new responsibility, such as becoming a pilot, I would test them to ensure that they were properly trained to step into that role. In essence, I was putting my life on the line every single day, testing and evaluating soldiers. It was pretty fascinating being a woman and leveraging so much power. As is usual for women, I had to face many situations in which I was underestimated and disrespected. Although I should have been accepted and celebrated, I was instead questioned and accused.

Have you ever been in a situation when you were confident in your abilities and your effort, yet had to fight and claw your way through? When although you knew the reality of the situation, you were still accused, threatened, and underestimated? Unfortunately, as women, and especially black women, we find ourselves in this position all too often. What do you do? You persevere.

You are stronger than you think you are. You have more tenacity and more confidence than people give you credit for. Do NOT allow them to stand in your way or hold you back! I didn't, and although my situation did not work out as I had thought, I did NOT back down.

My commanding officer, new to this particular unit, called me in to question my whereabouts. He accused me of being "lazy like the rest of the staff," as he said. Did he not understand that I *know* how to be a soldier? That I respect the uniform and all that it represents? He had to be kidding me with his accusations from his comfy office behind the protected barrier, while I risked my life every day outside in the real world of war for him under his command!

I am glad that I had the wherewithal to stay the course and stand firm in completing my responsibilities. I did not allow anyone, not even the commanding officer, to deter me from doing what I knew was right. Sometimes we have to do just that. Continue pushing forward when we know that it is right, even though we are faced with opposition and adversity. Don't allow other people to get in your way.

My immediate supervisor, the one that I had already encountered about the disrespectful officer, sat me down and had to finally admit the error in his ways and his thinking. He said, "A lot of people were wrong about you and I was one of them. I was really wrong about you and I wanted to tell you that." He continued saying that, "There are not a lot of good things that were said about you and I called up some of those people to tell them they were wrong. They were wrong because I couldn't do my job if it wasn't for you. I want you to know how much I appreciate everything you are doing. You get the highest accolades from me."

That conversation told me exactly what I knew in that season. I was supposed to stay the course. They had to respect that. At the end of the day, the jobs I had were critical because the unit couldn't function without the support I provided. My efforts were directly in support of the big commander and that entire area of operation. As a result, the commander came to our unit and acknowledged my efforts by awarding me the Combat Spur. It is one of the most prestigious honors one can receive for providing logistical support to a Cavalry unit. This honor afforded me the respect that I deserved all along. Even the officer who I had originally had an altercation with had to respect me for what I had done for the section.

During the winter season, when the wind is beating at your brow, you have to stay the course. Even if you are faced with oppression, discrimination, opposition, conflict - stay the course because at the end of it all, there is a reward and you will receive that reward both physically as well as mentally. On the other side of the winter, there are benefits.

As I was faced with all of these challenges, I kept repeating to myself, "Stay the course, stay the course." At the same time, I reflected on a time six years earlier when the doctors were afraid that I would not even make it out of surgery. My husband had disrespected me, yet I stayed the course. He was so concerned about going to war and it was ironic that ultimately, I was the one sent off to put my life on the line (again).

I had to have mental toughness through it all and rely on God to sho me that He is in control. I couldn't think about the adversity and the reality of the situation. I simply had to act with God as my stronghold, with courage in the face of adversity, through all of it. I had to have confidence in the abilities that God had given me: to not only hold my head up, but to stay alive so that I could come back to my children. This winter season brought out the best in me.

The winter season will bring things out of you that have been dormant. Even when the storms come, there will be a day when you don't have to put on that same winter coat. You don't have to put on that same armor. You will be equipped because God will deposit strength in you, and it will only rise to the surface when you need it the most.

## Autumn season

Before the winter season, we always have to go through the autumn season, when everything looks so beautiful but in fact, is near the end. This is a time in your life when things are coming to their end as well.

When I came back from Iraq, I know that it was the beginning of the end. I returned to the National Guard where I was comfortable and did not have to prove anything to anyone. I began submitting applications for my next position. I was introduced to a woman who would later become my mentor. As she reviewed my resume, although she was very impressed with my accomplishments, she gave me one word of advice – pliable. Although I didn't know what that meant at the time, I knew that in some way my intolerance of disrespect and my strong desire to do my job while maintaining my personal morals and ethics was going to come back to bite me.

Have you ever just known that the end was near? Did you ever experience that moment when you knew that the Holy Spirit was speaking to you and you should listen?

I was recommended for a position in command of a unit where there had been a lot of issues: DUIs, drugs, sexual assault, and even suicides. My competence in each of my roles had preceded me and my mentor suggested that I was the best person for this position. She had the confidence in me to take this position and truly make a difference, as I had done in so many of my roles before.

I approached this role as I have so many others. I identified what needed to be done, I surveyed the troops, and I acknowledged where the issues were. This unit was one of the first units to have been deployed in 2003, and I had trained some of these guys back then. There were a lot of young people, a lot of history and pain. They had seen their share of toxic leaders and lost some of their friends in the war. Coping with these tragedies was difficult for so many of these soldiers.

So, I did what I always do. I jumped right in and got to work.

My mentor and friend moved on to another position. The commander that took over was an individual with whom I had worked for before. He was a former Marine and more importantly, a misogynist. I knew he did not have respect for women, which led me further into my autumn season. Although I made tremendous progress in helping the soldiers and improving the overall state of that unit, at the end of the day, he accused me of proselytizing. Really? I didn't even know what the word meant.

In his words, I was using my religion to influence those in my command. Had I organized a retreat for singles with a chaplain? YES. Had I arranged for marriage counseling for couples and relationship counseling for singles? YES. Because apparently I used the word "GOD", I was pushing religion on the soldiers, which was allegedly offensive to some of the men in this unit. They felt I had violated their spiritual rights. According to statements, I was described as the following: " "She was okay. She got us trained but she wouldn't let us drink beer. She didn't let us have any fun." I was accused of using my position to preach God and force God on my soldiers. This situation was pushing my career to the end. Although the progress we were making looked beautiful, little did I know that this was the autumn season before my career in the military died.

I tried to tell my side of the story. I wrote letters to the head of the organization and launched a complaint of my own, which only served to lead into discrimination. Unfortunately, it wasn't the discrimination against me that was being brought up. No. The complaint was somehow viewed as me accusing the commander of being a racist. Interestingly, it was later revealed that some of the soldiers under my command didn't feel like they should have to salute a black woman. So, the truth finally came out. We were back to the struggles that many of us beautiful sisters have to deal with.

I had to get the NAACP involved. When they read the complaint, they knew the statements were wrong, but who was going to go back into this white organization and accuse anyone? The real issue was that I had too much power.

There are seven core values that are highly respected and define what it means to be a soldier in the U.S. Army: loyalty, duty, respect, selfless service, honor, integrity, and personal courage. As I said earlier, I know what it means to be a soldier and I take these values very seriously. To further discredit me and my service, the commander wrote an evaluation and said I needed to be relieved from command, stating that I was neglecting all of these values except one - courage. His claims were taken with a grain of salt, as my very expensive attorney said. It's almost ironic that he would say that I was courageous. According to him, I was disloyal, had no sense of duty, honor, or respect, yet I had recently returned from Iraq with a bronze star!

Autumn or Fall as it is more appropriately called, is just that, a fall. You may be doing good, working hard, and then you fall hard. They tried to make me fall from grace. It was a spiritual attack. The season itself represented a change in my position as well as in people's view of me. Things that should have been celebrated were not. In the end, I had been following a regulation in both the Army and National Guard - one that embraces resiliency and spiritual fitness. It is the commander's responsibility. I had not violated anyone's rights nor was I proselytizing. I didn't overstep any boundaries. I was simply ensuring spiritual fitness.

Ultimately, I had to walk away from my military career and retire. I had made the impact that I needed to make. My struggles had served a purpose and now my time was coming to an end. God assured me that He would still be with me. It wasn't about the accolades or a pat on the back. They were trying to tarnish my brand, trying to make my edges smooth. But God knew better; he knew and had given me the courage to stand up for myself and to the situation.

Can you think of a time when someone tried to dim your light? When your light was so brilliant that you scared people because of the greatness that they saw coming from you? Did you wither and shrink from the pressure or did you allow God's power and strength to flow even more freely to impact the situation?

## Spring season

Spring is a time of new birth, new beginnings. It is like the emergence of a beautiful butterfly as it spreads its wings for the first time. It starts with an understanding of why these things happen.

I'm not going to lie. I had a hard time after my career came to an end. I was a little hurt after having spent a lifetime serving my country. I was feeling sorry for myself and I couldn't see how life was going to turn around.

When I began looking for a job, my friend told me about a position training veterans. Really? She wanted me to go back to a military base where I had just experienced such betrayal? Heck no. Finally, she convinced me to go on the interview. I never could have imagined such an Amazing outcome.

I was offered the job of training veterans in the successful transition from military service back to civilian life. No matter the bad taste that I had in my mouth, I felt reinvigorated by the thought of helping others to build a resume, learn interview skills, help them get a job, and be prosperous. Little did I know that the job was going to be so healing.

For three years, I flew to various states and had the opportunity to meet Amazing people who had served their country and now had the opportunity of starting life again. Although I had been so resistant, I now thanked God for this refreshing rebirth. I understood why I had gone through all that I did. I was able to use my experiences to help other people heal, and the more I talked about it, the more it was healing for me. I spent 22 years in the military and was now receiving the blessing of being able to serve in a new capacity. Not only was I spreading my wings, but it was a ministry that God was using me to speak life into individuals. It was like a resurrection. I had so many participants in my class, especially the women who were beaten down and brokenhearted.

I could have been jaded by all of my experiences and, in the beginning, I think I was. But at this time in my life, this job was a blessing. I had been where they were and maybe where you are today as well. Maybe you are beaten down, downtrodden, brokenhearted. I was able to comfort these military veterans because of what I shared with them. It was refreshing and healing for them to have a military person that could relate to them. Although they would often tell me how amazed they were at my accomplishments, it was these brave, Amazing, brilliant veterans who deserved to be celebrated.

I hope that my stories and experiences serve to help you as much as they did these participants in my class. Know that you too can be inspired, you can emerge as a beautiful butterfly, just as I did.

I used to think it was somewhat condescending for people to say, "Thank you for your service." I shared that in many of my classes, but before I knew it, I was thanking them for their service. It was not about me. It was actually me seeing these people and being able to embrace and appreciate them. It was also about them feeling appreciated for what they had done. No matter what they did in the military, I found a reason to show them thanks and help them see how they should be celebrated for serving their country. You should be celebrated for your contributions to life as well.

God has a way of bringing things full circle. We walk through life and sometimes we can be very underappreciated and disparaged. There are so many things designed to keep us from knowing our value and true identity in Christ. We are supposed to prosper and be in good health, even as our soul prospers. We tend to be blocked and beaten down throughout our lives. We need to surround ourselves with people who remind us of who God says we are, who remind us of our value. We need to be able to say, "I was missing out on all of this greatness because of what people thought of me. I am special. I do matter. My voice does count." Sometimes it just takes us being thrust into those circles of encouragement for it to really be brought home.

# Summer season

When you go on vacation, you usually expect the sun to be shining. It's time to stretch, not stress yourself. It's time to slow down and appreciate things. The summer season is the time of summer love. My new husband represents the sunshine coming back into my life.

I knew I needed to put God first. When I got away from all of my shortcomings, this man came into my life like a ray of sunshine. He brought back laughter. I had gone through so much. I had been tense, too focused on everything being on point. Relaxation, smiling, and even laughter had been lost along the way. He reminded me and illuminated me again. As the saying goes, iron sharpens iron, or as some people say, "This person completes me." I wouldn't even say that he completes me but he brought his sunshine and made my light shine even brighter.

In this season of stretching, we built our home together as a sanctuary where we could sit back and relax. He built what I like to call my Garden of Eden in the backyard, which includes a hot tub and beautiful fruit trees, creating an enchanting, relaxing space.

In this place, the summertime, as the lights shine bright, everyone typically wants to show off. People want to show off their bodies. Spiritually, I would like to equate that to a place that I've learned how to be naked, vulnerable, and not ashamed. A place where there are no masks. A place where you do not have to worry about making mistakes. In the past, I have attracted people into my life for superficial reasons. My husband, he saw my heart. He embraced me, flaws and all.

It's a beautiful place to be partnered with someone that you can celebrate life with. We're in this beautiful place called retirement. What do we do next? We understand that there's a divine purpose and my life was designed for me to make an impact and know that now it's not about me. It's about giving, but not giving so much that it depletes me.

As I wrap up this chapter about the seasons of womanhood, I want to bring you back to how God sees all of us as women. While many people avoid Proverbs 31:10-31, believing that it is an unrealistic and unattainable standard for women, especially women of color, it tells me how God created women to be of noble character throughout all of the seasons of our lives. It is meant to encourage us to continue following God and reminds us that He will direct our path, the one that He has already laid out for us.

# Proverbs 31:10-31 New International Version (NIV)

The Wife of Noble Character

10 A wife of noble character who can find?

   She is worth far more than rubies.

11 Her husband has full confidence in her

   and lacks nothing of value.

12 She brings him good, not harm,

   all the days of her life.

13 She selects wool and flax

   and works with eager hands.

14 She is like the merchant ships,

   bringing her food from afar.

15 She gets up while it is still night;

   she provides food for her family

   and portions for her female servants.

16 She considers a field and buys it;

   out of her earnings she plants a vineyard.

17 She sets about her work vigorously;

   her arms are strong for her tasks.

18 She sees that her trading is profitable,

   and her lamp does not go out at night.

19 In her hand she holds the distaff

   and grasps the spindle with her fingers.

20 She opens her arms to the poor

   and extends her hands to the needy.

21 When it snows, she has no fear for her household;

   for all of them are clothed in scarlet.

22 She makes coverings for her bed;

   she is clothed in fine linen and purple.

23 Her husband is respected at the city gate,

where he takes his seat among the elders of the land.

24 She makes linen garments and sells them,

and supplies the merchants with sashes.

25 She is clothed with strength and dignity;

she can laugh at the days to come.

26 She speaks with wisdom,

and faithful instruction is on her tongue.

27 She watches over the affairs of her household

and does not eat the bread of idleness.

28 Her children arise and call her blessed;

her husband also, and he praises her:

29 "Many women do noble things,

but you surpass them all."

30 Charm is deceptive, and beauty is fleeting;

but a woman who fears the Lord is to be praised.

31 Honor her for all that her hands have done,

  and let her works bring her praise at the city gate.

# Chapter 4

# Faith Above Fear

God has always played a tremendous role in my life. Without knowing Jesus Christ as my Lord and Savior, I would not have been the strong woman that He made me to be. However, my faith journey has not always been easy.

As people, and even as women, we are tested. Our faith is stretched to the limits. Yet, through it all, know that God is and always will be your rock, your anchor. He will always show up when you need Him the most.

During my younger life, I had a different image of what being a Christian meant. What I understood the term "being saved" to be is different than how I understand it to be now. I know that there is a difference between religion and relationship and you can, in fact, have one without the other.

Let's pause there for just a second to let that soak in. You may be a church-going girl but do you have a relationship with God? Do you go to church each Sunday out of fear or because you truly have a relationship with the almighty Father? I guess that most people, like I did, have religion. I wanted a relationship.

Many of us grew up in the church, watching our prayerful Black mothers pleading with God for better circumstances, to be freed of the abuse, neglect, or burdens placed on them. We listened as they prayed, cried, and shouted out to God to change their lives, to give them strength, and to watch over their children. They were going to church to work through the pain of being a black woman in America. Watching this, we too turn to God for salvation and redemption. But again, is this a religion or relationship?

World renown, iconic singer and songwriter Beyoncé, as a Southern church girl, turns to what she knows best when life gets hard – to God and to church. She follows the rules and standards that she has been given through religion, just as her mother did before her saying, "Fasted for 60 days … confessed my sins and was baptized in a river. Got on my knees and said 'Amen' and said 'I mean'… I drank the blood and drank the wine. I sat alone and begged and bent at the waist for God … and plugged my menses with pages from the Holy Book.

But still inside me coiled deep was the need to know, are you cheating on me?"[ii]

In her new album "Lemonade", she calls Black women "to reimagine their relationships in intimate and social spaces through constructing a relationship with God that makes self-love primary. Their mothers brought them to the faith. Now it must become their own."

I always knew that I wanted to be better. I wanted to be my best self, like being a great wife. But I also knew that I couldn't do this without God.

That was my prayer. I needed God to show me how to show up as myself. But the way I went about it was misguided. Don't get me wrong, it is important to go to church, to read scriptures, and to be religious. But I needed more. I needed to really get down and have a relationship with God. I needed to speak to him privately and to tell him my deepest, most precious thoughts and fears.

Throughout all of the situations in my life, I have longed for and needed that deep relationship with God because I have always known that without Him, I could not become all that He designed me to be of my own free will. Without His guidance and strength, I just wasn't strong enough, bold enough, or courageous enough to live my life the way He intended.

Have you ever felt that way? Many people believe and pronounce that they are a Christian or that they have been saved. Unfortunately, many of them also rely on the strength of their religion to get them through. No. Real faith comes when you place all of your faith in God despite fear and uncertainty. Real faith happens when you place all of your trust in God and ask Him to give you the strength to make it through.

I think the first time that my faith was really stimulated was when Talil was born with spina bifida. At that moment, faith became real to me. I had not understood what it all meant until I was at the point where something so devastating happened to me and I knew I could not do it alone. I cried out in earnest, "Why, why God, why would this happen to me?" I didn't understand it then, but this is what formed the basis of my relationship with God. I finally understood that I can actually cry out to God whenever I need and want to. There is no protocol for when you speak to God or ask Him, "Lord, please help me."

There is a thought in religion that you should not question God. It took something quite devastating to happen for me to throw everything out the window. Everything I was taught about what it meant to have a relationship with God was no longer valid. That is when I crossed the threshold and finally understood how faith comes into play.

You don't know what you don't know. I didn't really have a heart for God. Now having a relationship with Him, I know that He already had plans for me. He chose me even when I didn't know that I was chosen.

Looking back on my life, everything that I have gone through had to happen. These things were destined to happen for me to learn and to get to where I am now. Your faith has to be tested. All the things that I yearned for in my heart, those things I fantasized about in my dreams, had to be tested. He chose me to be the vessel because I finally yielded my will to Him.

I had always talked with Him through prayer. I was going by a standard that other people had imposed on me, by the black mothers I saw at church. I thought I knew what it looked like to have a relationship with God. He allowed me to have these fantasies of what right looked like to me. Because I had these images in my head, the fairytales I created in my mind, I made mistakes. The truth of the matter is that I was too busy trying to wear the mask that I really didn't know who I was.

I can show up now as myself in other relationships because that's the relationship I have with God. I understand the Word because He helped me to see it. This is not to say that showing up as yourself and putting the mask down is always easy, especially when you are faced with adversity. When you experience challenges, who do you turn to?

Do you run to God with your problems or do you try to tackle them alone, wearing the mask and believing the lies that you have told yourself?

We all have those moments during our lives when we have to recommit our lives to God. We each have our own salvation experience. What was salvation like for you, dear reader? If you haven't yet experienced it, no worries. God is still with you.

I was baptized when I was about 12 years old, but I can't even say that I understood what I was doing at the time. I had this impression of what I thought religion was. But I always knew in my heart that I just wanted to please God. Even though I was doing all of those things that I thought would put me in His good graces, I still had questions. "Does God even hear me? Is He listening? Why is He not talking back?" I always wondered. I heard people saying that God talks to them, but He wasn't really talking to me. I was reading the Bible but I wasn't hearing anything back. I was still trusting and believing that I would. I just knew that there had to be something higher than me but it wasn't until Talil was born that I understood.

My spirit was awakened to another level. It was the moment when I really understood that God had sent us something special with the Holy Spirit and that I had been chosen to carry out something special, just not with my own mind or my own strength. I was going to need God's help to be able to help this little boy.

Have you ever reached that point when you just knew you had to reach out to something higher? You knew that you couldn't do it alone? What was that moment like for you?

When my twin sons were born, I was trying to understand and grapple with what they were telling me about Talil. He would not be able to move anything from his waist down. Then they came back to say he had to have his teeth removed because he was born with two teeth in his mouth. What in the world? I was numb. Have you ever felt so badly that you can't feel anything at all? I completely surrendered. The first time I went in to feed him I saw him on a board. His feet deformed. I couldn't touch him. I couldn't hold him. I had to pull the board up to me. Since he was close to 24 hours old, he was hungry. They really wanted him to eat and be nurtured by his mom. At first, I just sat there looking at him as he made this almost inaudible whimper. Then when I pulled him closer to breastfeed, my heart sank to my feet. But it was at that moment that I asked "Lord, please give me the strength."

I couldn't cry. I had to be strong for Talil. I had to rise above and see him beyond where I saw him at that moment. Here is this fragile little baby, wounded and afflicted. I needed to see and to trust God that this was a temporary situation. This too shall pass!

"This too shall pass." This is a foundational scripture in our faith journey. We all have experienced trauma in our lives and have gotten through it before. We have to remember during seasons of uncertainty, seasons of hurt and betrayal, that this too shall pass. Rely on your faith to lead and guide your decisions.

I have had to allow my faith and trust in God to guide my decisions and my perspective. After my divorce from Troy, moving on to another relationship seemed impossible. Moving past it was certainly easier said than done. There's a saying that the fear of a thing is greater than the thing itself. We all tend to create a fear in our mind of the worst-case scenario and then the feelings are developed from that. I had these feelings of inadequacy. I thought, "There's no way that after this I'm going to be able to pick myself up." I felt that there was no way I could give myself openly and freely to anybody else. I told myself, "I'm going to hold back some things." Even with my kids, I thought, "How do I now think about what's best for them?" You can think you are doing the right things for your kids, but sometimes you have to do what you know to do and not be so concerned about the outcome. Fear holds us back. In fact, you may fear the outcome so much that you don't do anything at all.

Doing nothing can actually make the situation worse. But I certainly did not understand this. All the things that I feared about moving on and moving on too quickly and being with somebody else were in my head. When I think about how the divorce really affected the kids, I think about my daughter. When my daughter Teryn got to the age that she was thinking about dating, it was really an emotional roller coaster for her. It hit me when she asked me the question, "What made you divorce dad? What made you want to get divorced?" I realized she was asking these questions because she wanted to date. Now that particular fear of the unknown was prevalent in her mind. "I love my mom and dad. Everything looked happy and then all of a sudden they are divorced."

We talked about our relationship and how happy I was now. I asked her if she would rather that we go back in time and change things back to what they were before. She realized how important happiness is and how sometimes you have to do what is necessary to be happy.

Sometimes we think we want something and what we want is not necessarily the best thing for us. That's why I think God gives us the desires of our hearts. He will give those things to us but then He also saves us from ourselves. I was so caught up in the stigma of being a single mother, a divorcee. Is it a sin to get divorced? I was thinking about the fairytale rather than knowing that God is bigger than all of those things.

Fear tends to rest on us. But through faith, you can rise above fear. You have to step out in faith and give your life a chance. It rests in the ability to forgive. We look at forgiveness as something for the other person when in fact, forgiveness allows us to move forward. I thank God for the gift I have of forgiveness which allows me not to focus so much on those things that happened to me but rather the place I am in now. I no longer look at myself as the victim allowing those things that happened to me to hold me back. God gives me the gift of moving on, of healing. Forgiveness lifts the burden so that you can see ahead beyond the shortcomings and failures.

The process is deep but simple. You must ask God to take the reins. You have to let go of the thought that you have to control everything in your life. I looked at my life and thought, "This is a mess. I'm getting divorced." But those are my eyes looking at it in a natural way rather than looking at it in the way that God sees it. I couldn't see all the learning and the growth that came out of that relationship. I can now see the beauty and great things that came out of it as both my husband and I are better off because of what we went through.

This concept of seeing life from a different perspective is relevant to our lives. You will be better off because of what you went through. You should not feel ashamed or feel blame. The process of forgiving will allow you to then walk into the newness of your life because of what you went through. If you don't forgive, you tend to be a victim which causes you to not live your best life.

I had come to understand what it really means to forgive and give myself another chance. I could have stayed in that marriage because I was forgiven and willing to give it another chance. But I can't overpower somebody else's will and I can't control the outcome. When things were made clear to me, that I wasn't his number one, I had to respect that as crazy as it sounds. Dealing with that is the same as a form of rejection.

God showed me that He allows us to follow our own will. We could stay in seasons longer than we need to, prolonging the suffering that is attached to it simply because we don't hear. But He wants us to open up our eyes and see what's going on. Sometimes it's hard to see things that you don't want to see. I knew if I opened my eyes and saw what was going on around me in my marriage, I'd have to do something different. I finally realized that this was not a reciprocal relationship in which we both received and gave respect. I had to finally open my eyes, pick myself up, and do something different.

Despite the test of your faith, you will overcome. No matter what it is that you may be experiencing, you will overcome it through faith. Faith over fear will prevail and lead you to the life that God intended for you to have.

"Fear can render us useless for God's purposes if we allow it to." Lisa Brown, speaker, mom, grandma, writer, pastor's wife, and 3-time cancer survivor shares that FEAR is, in fact, a four-letter word that can paralyze us if we let it. After being told for the third time that she was again faced with cancer eating away at her body, she decided that she would no longer allow fear to dictate her life. She finally prayed to God to take the fear from her. While she had been asking Him to let her see another day, then another year with her children and be free from cancer, she realized that by releasing her fear to Him was more powerful than any cancer treatment or surgery. She had to live by faith alone in that God would take care of her no matter the outcome.

Lisa is now cancer-free living the life that God intended for her. She has learned to rely on His Amazing promise of peace and faith over fear as scripture tells us in Philippians 4:7, "And the peace of God that transcends all understanding will guard your hearts and minds in Christ Jesus."

Trust me, my sisters, when I tell you that through faith over fear, you will walk side by side with God in the life that He intended for you to live.

# Chapter 5

# Circle of Trust

The goal for all of us is to become the best version of ourselves. We cannot do this and tackle such a feat by ourselves. We all need a community, a circle of trust to help us. We need the right people in our environment to help us through.

I have experienced a lot of fear in my life. When the twins were born, I had the other young kids at home as well. So, my mom came out to live with me for a little bit to help out. It was Amazing for me to have that opportunity to mend things that she and I had dealt with, or better stated, didn't address, in the past. The whole time she was speaking life over me. She told me how much she admired me and how strong she thought I was. When I had my surgery, she was instrumental in my healing and ability to remain calm. Before the doctor came in, I had a conversation with her over the phone and she said, "Stop! Something doesn't sound right. I want to pray with you because you're not sounding right."

I didn't know what she was talking about at the time, but she could hear it in my voice. Whatever it was, she knew that this was a time to intercede and pray. She spoke encouraging words to me. "You're going to make it through this. This is yet another thing that's going to pass. You're going to get through this. The doctors know what they're doing. You've got this host of support." After the surgery, she flew out and helped to take care of me and to help with the children so that I could focus on healing.

When I was young, I didn't appreciate things about her that as an adult I now really appreciate. For example, her toughness. I understand now that her tough love growing up laid foundations for me. That was the baseline for me to be who I am. The resiliency that I have came from that seed that she planted in me long ago.

My circle of trust had always been fairly small. I kept a community of close confidantes tightly around me and very rarely allowed others in. But, as women, we all need that close-knit community of others to help and support us. I did allow another woman into my circle as part of my support system. Through our work together in the military, my friend and confidant Maureen Peltier has been by my side throughout so many struggles and challenges. When I was accused of proselytizing, she stood by me. When they tried to relieve me of my duty, she fought for me as an activist.

Our relationship is built upon mutual respect and trust. Every woman needs someone in her life who can be brutally honest with her as well as with whom she can share her deepest secrets. When we met, Maureen had been working in the unit over which I had command. She was tired and military life had taken a toll on her. Her competency and reputation had preceded her and I knew that I was fortunate to have her on my team.

After a brief conversation early in my command, I told Maureen I would call her in a few days. True to my word, I called her two days later. She was shocked that I had actually done as I had said when so many others had let her down in her life. It wasn't until sometime later in our friendship that Maureen revealed to me that I had saved her life that day. She had been in so much emotional pain and attempted suicide twice before; she decided once again that day she was going to kill herself. But hearing my voice and knowing that I really cared and followed up with her, she knew that I was unlike any of the others in a leadership position. It was then that she decided that life was worth living. I thank God for Maureen's decision that day and for her friendship and dedication to me over the years. She has truly saved my life as well. I know that God placed her within my circle of trust for a unique purpose and I in hers as well.

When I needed Maureen, she advocated and fought for me, even jeopardizing her own military career to work on my behalf. She took my story to the national level, writing about the injustice that was happening to me. Her commitment was so intense that the officer who had filed the original complaint against me now had a new plan of attack. He accused me of having an inappropriate relationship with one of my soldiers (Maureen), simply because he could not understand how someone could so passionately advocate on my behalf. He could not understand the circle of trust and community of support that women have and the glue that binds us together.

Do you have a circle of supporters who you know, beyond the shadow of a doubt, that you can rely on? Someone who you trust implicitly to have your back, who would advocate for you if you needed? Does anyone in your life know that they can rely on you during times of struggle, pain, and distress? Take this time to evaluate your circle of trust. When you expose your authentic self, flaws and all, it's really important to have people around you who can be there to validate, comfort, and console you.

The encouragement that you receive from those people who love you helps you to understand and to see things that you wouldn't have normally seen. Every one of us needs that support system to help us grow. I'm very grateful and thankful to Maureen for her help and for providing me with the opportunity to grow.

At the end of the day, everything revolves around me being whole in every state. Another person who is an integral part of my circle of trust is my husband. As the closest relationship to me, my husband's trust was jeopardized when I divorced my first husband. My husband now tells me regularly that he admires my beauty and my strength. He speaks encouraging words over me which help me to keep moving forward.

Both my mom and Maureen became a part of my support system by Divine intervention. But there are some intentional strategies that every powerful woman can and should use to create a circle of trust of those people that can uplift them.

My strategy is that everything starts with your nucleus. It has to be healthy at the core, otherwise, it jeopardizes every relationship after that going forward. Within the relationship that I have with my husband now, there is accountability. Yes, he wants to see me successful but he's not afraid to let me know if I stray from my course. He's there to cover me in those areas where I'm weak and I need to grow in. At the same time, he provides a level of protection. It wasn't just me as a soldier who put her career on the line. He was still serving in uniform and actually had to put his whole career on the line as well. He voluntarily retired because of what was happening to me. He became a voice piece advocating against the attacks that came against me.

He was the reinforcement that I needed to get back up on my feet. He lifted me up emotionally after my divorce. We worked together and professionally, he knew of my work ethic and determination. He had noticed that I was working long hours and was burning the candle from both ends. I was leaning toward success and not recognizing that I needed support.

He stepped in, not in an invasive way, but in a way to offer help. I remember a time when he stepped in as just a friend to help me when I was working late, but rushing to get home to celebrate my ex-husband's birthday. He didn't have an ulterior motive but went and purchased a gift for him from the kids and I. He even went so far as to pick up a cake! He was just looking out for my well-being as a true friend and supporter. My husband loved all of the gifts, so much so that he put on the new outfit and went out. I didn't see him for three days.

I can laugh about it now. That was just a prelude into my relationship with my new husband. He genuinely cared and was there for me even before things escalated into a romantic relationship. He does a lot for me just because it is in his nature. He is a blessing to me and has shown me that the fairytale that I always imagined was not just a fantasy. I believed then that it was possible but then was let down and deflated by reality. He has shown me, and should be a moniker to other women, that the fairytale life that you envision is possible. You have to put your trust in God, trust and believe in yourself, and allow Him to guide your every move.

As my husband, my friend, my confidant, he was able to step in when I needed him the most, even before the intimacy took place. As women, we can have relationships all around us, but it's all about tapping into them and knowing how to access the help when we need it. A lot of times we're strong and we're brave and we're used to showing up for everyone else but it is difficult to be able to say, "Yes, I actually need help."

As corporate women, it may be difficult to let down our guard to ask for help. But, to be resilient, to become the best possible versions of ourselves, we often have to be kind to ourselves, forgive, and show ourselves mercy. There is tremendous power in self-forgiveness. This is an area in which we all need to continuously grow. Without forgiving yourself, it leaves out the potential to be better. You can be stuck there being a victim.

There's a freedom that comes with forgiveness and a lot of times we associate forgiveness with a feeling when it's not. It's an act of moving forward. Forgiving yourself is the hardest thing because feelings get in the way. Your emotions get in the way of how you feel about the situation, especially when you feel wronged. We all tend to want to express that or want to be vindicated or set straight for that. We've talked about seasons before and there's definitely a time and a season for everything.

The power of forgiveness is not really dismissing the fact that bad has happened. It's still there. I hate the phrase "fake it till you make it" because faking it till you make it implies that it's a segue into putting a mask on. "I can't ever make this, so I have to pretend to be something else." That's not the truth. Whatever the thing is, whatever the hurt, I believe you should not rely on "fake it till you make it", but rather *face* it till you make it. So, you have to face that pain. It is key to have a trusted circle of people around you. When you forgive yourself, it opens up that circle for these people that God has allowed around you to create a safety zone where there is no judgment.

You need people around you to embrace you, who want to see you be the best you that you can be, and to love you for that. Forgiveness opens up the window and the vision for the future. Until you actually forgive, you're stuck in that story, at that moment. You can't see beyond and you can't see anything else to move forward. The act alone of forgiving lets you go forward.

One of the things that I feared about moving forward, especially after the divorce, was forgiving myself for my negative thoughts about having a broken home. The fear wasn't what I thought for me, but as a parent thinking about my kids. I disrupted their lives. How could I forgive myself for that? By forgiving myself, I was not only able to move on but it freed me to be able to allow my new husband into my life.

I thought the only person that ideally could love my children as much as I or be there for them would be their biological father. I questioned, "How do I bring somebody else in my life that will love and accept my kids?" When you're in a fog, reality is tainted by the lies and stories that we tell ourselves. Those poisoned feelings caused by the hurt and the pain of the relationship were carrying over into all areas of my life. Until you forgive and cut ties with those feelings, your vision is going to be blurred.

One thing that helped shape me and helped me understand the importance of surrounding myself with positive people was when I was introduced to Zumba.

I was in an autumn season of my life, heading into winter. I was being forced to leave the military and had to figure out what my next moves were going to be. I love music and I love to dance and a close friend of mine invited me to participate in an exercise class. I had no idea what it was but quickly found out that it is like a party. Women from all walks of life were having a great time, dancing, partying, AND losing weight. Although at first I was skeptical, I realized that no matter where you are in life or what you look like or what shape you are in, Zumba is an Amazing way to get in some invigorating exercise and meet great people. It was a place that we could all come, flaws and all, and just be ourselves. It was a judgment-free zone that became more than just a workout for me.

This group of women were all just having fun. Although I was timid about it, I soon was able to let go and be myself too. Eventually, I got so confident in my abilities that I became a Zumba instructor. Yes. This seasoned military powerhouse was now motivating other women through dance. Sometimes I envision God sitting back having a good chuckle as he lays out the plans for our lives. Little did I know that these women would soon become an integral part of my circle of trust. They became my friends, my confidantes, and traveling buddies.

There are a lot of professional women in challenging, powerful positions doing Zumba. Women who are not only looking to relax and exercise but also looking for that bond with other women. My husband and I started hosting wine nights at our home. Since he is an Amazing cook, my friends loved and enjoyed an evening out at my house with good wine, good food, and good company. These nights offered all of us a safe place to get together as women, to let our hair down, to talk and share, get encouragement, and learn from one another.

We did everything we could to help one another, even providing opportunities to network and earn some money. We even invited some of the women with businesses to set up shop during our evenings together. For example, maybe a masseuse would do 15-minute massages or a foot scrub. It was a great opportunity that afforded each of us to get something out of it, whether it was to build a community, to make money, or just to fellowship.

As women, we need to support one another. Whether you have a business or know someone who does, bring them into your circle and help one another. What resources do you have available that could just make you feel young again, make you feel free again? Self-care is so important for not only physical health, but mental and emotional health as well. Support someone else by opening up opportunities for them. We are all in this together and must do what we can to support each other.

Zumba helped me establish this core team of females that I now consider to be within my circle of trust. We were professional women who just wanted a safe place to not feel judged, not to have to make decisions but to learn from one another and share resources. During this time, I was serving as a board member of a local Nonprofit, Northwest Leadership Foundation (NLF). It was an organization that existed to encourage, strengthen, and develop leadership for the spiritual and social renewal of the city. Subsequently, the CEO of NLF nominated me for membership to another local organization called American Leadership Forum (ALF) - Fellows Program. It was an honor to be selected for that group. Individuals select you or you get nominated by someone that has observed your leadership potential. They nominate you as a person who has demonstrated a lifetime of leadership qualities in different areas or capacities during their career. I accepted the nomination and I am now a part of a class of 23 other professional individuals (fellows), male and female, from different sectors of the community. We participate in a cohort for 18 months, getting to know each other, and learning from each other the roles of leadership, how to interact with one another, and share resources. This has also helped me to develop relationships with people who I can now say are part of my inner circle.

Even now during the global pandemic, we get together via Zoom meetings twice a week. At the beginning of each call, we have what's called a check-in. During the check-in period, everybody gets an opportunity to talk uninterrupted and everybody else just listens. The check-in is designed to see where you are and if you are present at the moment. If you're not, why not? What's going on? True accountability. There is also an established order or rules of confidentiality. No matter what it is, everybody else's job, other than the person that's talking, is to actively listen. Not to give any comments, or respond, but just actively listen. It is our job to indiscriminately listen and let that person pour it out. Each person has this moment when the community of people is listening, you feel the love, and are connected as you feel the support of the group.

I was able to branch out and find those things that brought me joy. Each of us needs that outlet, that means of discovering ourselves and what makes us happy. Be unafraid to try even when you are afraid. What is your outlet?

Everyone needs a support system that they can rely on, trust, and commit to. We all need friends and professionals that we can include in our circle of trust. If you do not have this trusted group of supporters, do not worry. You just haven't met the right people yet. God brings people into your life for a reason, a season, or a lifetime. He will bring you those people when you need them most to help guide, encourage, and support you.

In a world that rejects who we are as Black women at every turn, we must surround ourselves with those people who will lift us up, cheer us on, and mentor us. We battle with ourselves, against society, stereotypes, expectations, and stigmas. Ify Walker, the founder of The Offor Walker Group, an executive search firm, relies heavily on what she calls her "Lean In" circle of black women who support her as mentors, role models, and friends. She explains, "We are so powerful when we work together and so often that's not the narrative out there about black women. I might be the only person sitting in the room, but I'm not alone. I bring my army of supporters with me in spirit."[iii]

Who will you include in your circle of trust?

# Chapter 6

# Amazing Grace

The greatest challenge for me is showing up as my true, authentic self, relinquishing all control. I have no control over the situation or over the outcome, but I do have control of how I show up and what I do when I show up. I think a lot of women, like me, are caught up in perfectionism. We have to get everything right and have all the answers, know everything. I'm relinquishing that type of control because I'm not God. So, what is my job? My job is to motivate myself, not elevate myself above God. Sometimes we try to elevate ourselves to a status that we think that we should be able to accomplish, rather than the things that God has determined are for us.

I have written this book not only for you, my sister, my daughter, my friend. I have also written it for myself. Within the lessons that I have learned, there is always the thread of accountability. This book and my experiences continue to serve as my motivation and reminders that the lessons I learned throughout the challenges in my life were not for naught. It helps me to look back reflectively and say, "It was because you weren't perfect in the other situation that you're able to do this now." It was those things that I thought were plaguing me and those things that were bad that were the themes that pushed down on me and pressured me to actually be more creative.

There's a song about an olive that I love called *Greater is Coming*. An olive goes through three stages; the shaking, the beating, and the pressing. I can relate to these things. If not for these things that shook my foundation, the opposition that beat me down, and the seasons that pressed the weight of the world on to me, I couldn't be who I am today and who I was meant to be.

When I'm at my worst, feeling defeated, I get in my car and I blast that song. The process that the olive goes through is like the purification process that gold goes through. When we look at life, we are all shaken, beaten, and pressed. I was literally a diamond in the rough. A diamond has many cuts and colors that distinguish one from the other. Each diamond is unique and everybody wants a unique one of a kind gem. We are each unique, with our own cuts, having been shaken, beaten, and pressed. When diamonds are appraised, they have to be looked at from a certain light. Jewelers are looking for all those unique cuts; how the light shines off defines how that particular diamond faced the pressure beneath the earth being shaken, beaten, and pressed.

This book and the legacy that it represents are like the olive. It's a way that I can share my journey of being shaken, beaten, and pressed down. It helps to take away the guilt, shame, and blame that we as women naturally carry with us. Nobody can take away the things that have happened to me nor would I want them to. Each one has helped to shape me into the person that I have become, the woman that God intended for me to be. When I look at this book and how my life has played out, it allows me to know that I'm not in full control. God is in control and my job is to show up willing and able.

I have to be in this place just listening. I have to be in perfect peace within myself so I can be of service to God. Being of service to Him helps me serve myself as well as others. My son Talil wants to go out and save the world and help everybody else. I told him that we all have to be a service to ourselves first. If you can't be of service to yourself, get yourself shined up and cleaned up and allow God to let you see who you are and let the light first come from within you. Otherwise, it will be difficult for that light to shine through you.

I'd like to compare this book to the powerful message expressed in the movie Akeelah and the Bee in which 11-year-old Akeelah studies for and participates in the Scripps National Spelling Bee. The story inspires us to overcome obstacles despite challenges that we face along the way. It brings light to the issues that we as Black women face in our communities, leading to issues with our self-esteem, self-worth, and the lies that we tell ourselves. Akeelah faces her greatest fears and ultimately is victorious. We must show up to face our own greatest fears.

What is holding you back from being the best version of yourself?

Marianne Williamson, spiritual activist, author, and founder of the Peace Alliance, said it best when she wrote in her book *A Return to Love*, "Our deepest fear is not that we are inadequate but rather that we are powerful beyond measure. It is our light, not our darkness, that most frightens us. We ask ourselves, 'Who am I to be brilliant, gorgeous, talented, fabulous?' Actually, who are you *not* to be? You are a child of God. Your playing small doesn't serve the world."[iv]

In knowing that power, there comes great responsibility. It's easy to get caught up in the knowledge and power that we all possess. I thank God for the balance and humility which keeps me grounded to acknowledge that "I'm nothing without God." That's the faith journey. I don't know what tomorrow will bring, but I do know that I have control over how I show up for today. That's the choice I get to make in my life.

My message is not for everyone, but it is for you. My sister, I want to help you to find your voice. I hope that by sharing my imperfections something has ignited in you to show up more boldly and brilliantly than ever before because you've discovered new courage in your authenticity.

After all, if God is for you, who can be against you?

# EPILOGUE

After 11 years of marriage, my husband Lorenzo and I are living our best lives as retired "empty nesters."

We've come to understand that it's not about balance (50/50) in a relationship; balance is a misnomer.

It's more about maintaining harmony on any given day –
some days (70/30) and some days (60/40).

We're stronger than we've ever been.
After the completion of this book, I'm excited to add entrepreneur

to my resume. "Amazing Amy Lifestyles" is a venture designed
to offer health and emotional wellness opportunities for women to

help them achieve and maintain a healthy lifestyle.

One of the key ingredients to avoiding "imposter syndrome" is
removing "the mask" and to tapping into the feeling that "I am Enough"

on a daily basis, which is what  Amazing Amy Lifestyles will help you to do.

As for the other important people in my life …

Talil decided at 21 that it was time to gain his own independence.
I applaud him for venturing out on his own to experience life as a young black man living in this world; giving himself the opportunity to discover what it's like to cope with a disability. Talil is learning how to navigate the challenges of life, to respect his limitations, and exercise his ability to grow and develop into a productive member of society. At the same time, it is tough to watch him make mistakes, however, I never resist the opportunity to gently remind him that everything he desires is within his control. Talil has found refuge in expressing himself through music. He is an Amazing artist! With an Amazing gift to reach others through his messages of rap. I remind him daily that...HE IS ENOUGH.

Treyon (Talil's identical brother) will be completing his Master's in Education at the University of Washington (UW) in Spring 2021.

Amber – I maintain hope & reserve space for my "little girl" Amber. I hope that I have imparted some  wisdon into her life that reminds her of what it means to be loved by someone – even though

 I am not her biological mother.  It was important to me that I

provide her some semblance of hope that she can achieve and

maintain a healthy lifestyle to move forward, no matter what.

She is destined for greatness and will become a phenomenal woman.

Love,

Amy

This book was published with the support
of The Bestsellers Academy.

Do you have a book on the inside of you?

Let us get your story out of your belly and into an international
bestselling book!

Phone: 1-868-374-7441

Email: success@thebestsellersacademy.com

Website: TheBestsellersAcademy.com

# References

i https://www.huffpost.com/entry/imposter-syndrome-racism-discrimination_l_5d9f2c00e4b06ddfc514ec5c

ii https://religionandpolitics.org/2016/06/28/beyonces-lemonade-and-black-christian-womens-spirituality/

iii https://ssir.org/articles/entry/black_bold

iv https://www.vox.com/culture/2019/7/30/20699833/marianne-williamson-our-deepest-fear-nelson-mandela-return-to-love

Made in the USA
Columbia, SC
26 September 2021